Animals of the Arctic Tundra: Polar Region Wildlife

SPEEDY
PUBLISHING

Speedy Publishing LLC
40 E. Main St. #1156
Newark, DE 19711
www.speedypublishing.com

Arctic tundra is found almost entirely in the Northern Hemisphere.

The polar bear are the world's largest land predators. Polar bears spend most of their time at sea. They primarily eat seals.

Arctic fox is small animal that can reach 26 inches in length. Their hearing is so good that they can locate the exact position of their prey under the snow.

Caribou is a large mammal. It can reach 240 to 700 pounds in weight. Caribou releases special scent when faced with danger, it informs other caribous about near danger.

Arctic hares are the largest hares. Arctic hares have black eyelashes that protect their eyes from the sun's glare, just like sunglasses.

Snowy owls hunt actively during both day and night and are thus called, diurnal. They stay warm as their feathers do not have any pigments which leaves more room for air.

Musk oxen are herbivores. These arctic animals have thick hair that grows 2 feet long and almost touches the ground. They can weigh as much as 850 pounds.

Arctic Wolves live in very cold climates sometimes reaching -30 degrees. Arctic Wolves have two layers of very white fur to protect them against the cold temperatures.

Made in the USA
Middletown, DE
28 February 2022

61943956R00020